The Veneration of Life

*Through the Disease
to the Soul*

Other Books by Dr. John Diamond:

The Veneration of Life

Through the Disease
to the Soul

and

The Creative Imperative

John Diamond, M.D.

ENHANCEMENT BOOKS
Bloomingdale, Illinois

Cover photograph by John Diamond

The Veneration of Life: *Through the Disease to the Soul*

Copyright ©2000 John Diamond, M.D.

Published by: Enhancement Books
                 P.O. Box 544
                 Bloomingdale, IL   60108

ISBN 1-890995-14-2

To the memory of my mother,

Doris Diamond

1909-1993

I learned from my mother
in her demented, dying years,
that there's another plane
of existence.

Couldn't think,
couldn't speak –
approaching death –
but she radiated
the pure essence
of Life.

$\mathcal{T}$his little book is a summary of my over forty years of experience in psychiatry, complementary medicine, and holism. I have concentrated on the elderly for their needs are the most pressing. But I use them mainly as examples. Their problems are just the same as mine, and as yours, only highlighted.

Everything I say about them applies equally as fittingly to everyone. For none of us are blessed with True Health. And by attempting to help the elderly to achieve It, hopefully we will also find It for ourselves – earlier.

Through my mother's disease I came to know her as Spirit. The name of her disease hardly matters – no more than the name of the disease of your loved one. What matters is seeing through the disease to the sufferer's very essence, to their Soul.

I look upon my experience with my mother's Alzheimer's disease as an emblem, not of the relationship between health and disease, but of the True Health that lies through the disease and beyond. This perspective, which I am grateful to have received, I now offer to you.

The Veneration of Life

*Through the Disease
to the Soul*

Each of us has a special place inside us where we house our most treasured memories. I call mine my Inner Temple and in it I have three images of my mother.

The first was when I was quite young, and so was she. We sat on the grass in the park and made daisy chains for each other. My second, and the more precious, is as she lay dying in her final coma which was coming at last to her in Alzheimer's disease.

The first image is easy to understand, but why the second? Why, after so many years of increasing dementia, of seeming utter uselessness, would I hold on to this image? Because there is something very special about Alzheimer's disease – if we look at it other than in the usual way.

I know that my chances of getting Alzheimer's are higher than most, and I have often pondered deeply on whether I would want to be put to death if I developed it, being very aware, very aware indeed, of the suffering that it causes the family. And it is to them that I want to offer a different message.

To help the family not only to accept the disease in their loved one, but even, to an extent, to be grateful for it. So that when the loved one dies, as with my mother, the passing will be felt as a great loss. Not because of who the person was when well – but also, in fact even more, for Who they became through their illness.

This is the positive message I wish to give the relatives, so that they may be helped by their loved one's illness as I was greatly helped by my mother's. And I hope they, too, may now be helped by my mother's illness – so that her help to me carries on to others.

So would I want to be put to death if I had Alzheimer's? My answer used to be Yes – until I realized how much my mother and I were both transformed by her illness.

Now the answer for me would be No – for me and my family. I know only too well the anguish as the Alzheimer's takes hold and the poor sufferer realizes what is happening.

And I know, too, the anguish of the family and their mental suffering, and their financial burden. But at this stage of my enlightenment, I believe the benefits for them may well transcend their hardship.

As my mother lay dying, the nurses and aides would come in softly, reverentially, to say good-bye to her. Many of them gave her a kiss. One also stroked her hair and speaking, as much to my mother as to me, confided "She was such a sweet person." Yes, as I saw her in her Alzheimer's, that is what she was – and more. And More.

And there is a third image which is special to me. There was a time when she was very far gone, so they said, into her dementia. But I sat in front of her with my wife-to-be, Susan, whom she had never known before her illness – and by all usual criteria did not know now, no more than she, by similar criteria, knew me, or herself. And yet she took my hand in one of hers and Susan's hand in her other – linking us, deeply, permanently for life.

It is this image that has sustained us through the vicissitudes of our relationship. And most of all it was her eyes: we both looked into her eyes and she would look into mine and then into Susan's. And from her Soul through her eyes, she said everything. We were blessed by her love. We have lived since in her Belovedness.

$\mathcal{A}$lzheimer's is distinguished from most other diseases in that the ego becomes progressively smaller, allowing more and more of the innate Spirit to become apparent.

In contrast, nearly all diseases are characterized by an increased self-concern. In fact, this may very well be at the root cause of the particular disease. As the patient surrenders to the disease, he becomes increasingly more ego-oriented, radiating ever less of his Spirit.

So a basic therapeutic approach must be to help him to look outward and to give, for altruistic service can actuate the Therapeutic Power within him which alone can cure.

Nonetheless, the Spirit will always be there to be discerned through the ego. And the more that it is appreciated and encouraged, the greater the benefit for the patient and the relatives.

This is the new perspective, not just on Alzheimer's, and not on just illness – but on All of Existence.

Thus, what I have written may be a help to all those in suffering and their relatives, regardless of the particular diagnosis.

$\mathscr{T}$he summation of my clinical work over the last forty years has been that the only way we can overcome the suffering of our existence is to come to the realization that we each have a Spirit, a Soul, and that each of us is inherently, innately, Perfect.

The only way we can find the Spirit within each of us is to first find it in another. And the most significant others are our parents, most of all our mothers, but our fathers as well. Ultimately, before we can see ourselves as Spirit, we must so see our parents.

I had great difficulties with my parents, seeing them as anything but Spirit, anything but Love. To understand them, and to help me with them, was the reason I went into psychiatry. But I did not find the answer there. And I never found it, at least so far, with my father who died before I was ready.

But I believe I did find it with my mother, and for this I will always be grateful. Through her illness, because of her illness, I came to see her ever more clearly as Spirit. And so did the nurses.

They called her a sweet person, but at that stage she had long since ceased to be what we normally regard as a person. But she was still a Soul on earth even though her Spirit would be leaving soon.

Emerson wrote that there is, what he called, an Over-Soul, and that each of us has, as it were, a fragment of That which is our individual Soul. And I believe that the reason for our existence is to enable the Soul within us to progress, to mature and develop through this lifetime. And the more clearly we see this, the more we can help the Soul within us, and the Souls within others.

I came to understand my mother's psycho-pathology through my psychiatry. But I came to understand the Spirit, the highest attribute of our existence, from my mother in her dementia.

Through her illness I believe, hopefully, that I found my Soul. But what of her?

It is one of the great teachings that the Soul comes into physical existence in the body to act out the Way of its life: the work that needs to be done to help It on Its passage until It is finally completely evolved.

In the light of this teaching it can be said, that every illness, in fact every situation, can be, and indeed is, essential for the maturation of the Soul.

And so it was with my mother's disease. With her increasing dementia, her Soulhood, her Perfection, became ever more manifest, until at the end she was barely anything but pure Soul.

Perhaps it will be the Way of my life, that for the benefit of my Soul, I, my ego, will also decay with the ravages of the disease – but my Soul will progress through it.

The Soul, the Perfection within, is in a sense, imprisoned within the ego. The Soul, as the Muse, has a constant message of love which it yearns to manifest into the world. But it has no means whereby it can do this except through the aegis of the ego. And unfortunately, the ego very often misinterprets and misprocesses the Muse message.

My work now, since I had my enlightenment through my mother's illness, is to help sufferers to see past the ego misprocessings of themselves, and of others – and especially of their parents – to see the Perfection that is within. And to help them to realize the Spirit, and then to help them to express, to release, Its message of love into the world. The central core of this is surrendering the ego to the Soul within.

This is accomplished in Alzheimer's disease, although by destructive neuropathology. The dementia is a result of the disease eating away the ego, tragically not its voluntary surrender. And as increasingly more ego is destroyed, increasingly more Spirit becomes revealed. For the Spirit can never be destroyed. Rather It becomes more and more revealed into the world, so that increasingly the Muse message of love is now manifest.

But we have to learn how to find It, for the ego can no longer assist. No longer can the mother say "I love you, I've always loved you and I always will." But it is there to be heard – if only we will listen in a different way.

Every time I visited my mother in the nursing home I saw, I felt, I Knew, her Soul ever more closely, ever more lovingly, as her dementia increased. Previously, throughout our lives together, I had never been able to look into my mother's eyes. Now I could – not just into them – but deeply into them for they truly were the windows of the Soul. They were as pools of infinite peace.

Whenever I looked into them, it was as if I was transported to some other world, to the Land of Belovedness. I would hold her hands and gaze into her eyes and Know her, the Spirit that animated her, still. And I knew that she Knew me, the real me, the inner me. We knew each other as Souls. Thus did I find my mother's Soul, and thus through hers, my own.

One pure unselfish love
I found in my mother's eyes.

L. WOLFE GILBERT

As my mother sank progressively deeper into Alzheimer's, it was only her ego that died away, revealing her Soul ever more clearly. Until, at the end, that was all she was.

Every day I think of one time I visited her with my wife, Susan. She became almost obsessed with Susan's bunions which were nearly the same as hers. She would stroke them over and over.

Perhaps it was just that, in her demented state, she thought they were hers. But that is unlikely, for I never saw her stroke her own.

And there was more to it. Every time she touched Susan, she would then look up at me, straight into my eyes, my pupils. As if to say, "Johnny dear, Susan is me and I am Susan. Love us both as one."

She then took my hand in one of hers and Susan's in her other. And alternately she looked us in the eyes. And I, and Susan, saw into hers, deep into them.

Now when with a sufferer, I imagine my mother holding me with one hand and him with her other, as she did Susan.

We become linked, Soul to Soul, through my mother's Soul.

*F*reud wrote of what he called the Eternal Eros, the drive for love, in the most altruistic sense of that word. It is this that is most revealed as the ego is stripped away, and this persists until the very end.

And the greatest expression of it is Maternal Love – and This I saw in my mother not too long before her passing when I brought her baby great-grandson during my visit.

She had been sitting immobile for hours, for days and weeks, months – indefinitely – in one of those horrid rubber chairs that causes the body to contract even more than the disease itself. I was told that she hadn't spoken for so long – no one believed that she could speak.

And yet as soon as she saw the baby her eyes lit up, the Eternal Eros was actuated – highly! She reached out – as I knew she had towards me when I was a baby. She cradled him in her arms – as I knew she had me. And she stroked his head, still almost bald – as she had mine.

And then she repeated to him over and over in the most gentle lilting, loving way, "Little Darling, little Darling, little Darling." As I Know she had done with me.

All of her love, her Spirit, her Eternal Eros, manifested at that epiphanic moment. In that horrid chair she radiated her glorious numinosity. How could I ever doubt that she had a Soul?

How could I ever doubt that I had one when she had so loved me?

I brought her a doll, a little girl, for I knew that she always wished she had a daughter. By the time of her death, the little doll beside her bed had been so stroked that it, too, was now nearly bald. Was it just the result of the actions of a repetitive meaningless gesture – or was she revealing her Eternal Eros over and over?

$\mathcal{M}$usic takes a long time to die, for it too comes so directly from the Soul. I would take recordings to her – the very same ones I used to listen to when I was young. And as I played them to her she would become alive. Her eyes would brighten, and her Soul become even more apparent.

We would sing with her and she would respond with her eyes. We would wheel her out onto the lawn and sing and play the castanets. And I knew that she knew. It was Soul to Soul – mutual, reciprocal.

There was a time when we were dancing with her and Susan asked her, "Do you like dancing, Doris?" From deep within herself – and she hadn't spoken, we were told, for many months – she suddenly exclaimed brightly and clearly, looking Susan right in the eyes – at the top of her voice – "It's marvelous!" Yes, the music was still there – and More.

When I was six I was admitted to hospital extremely ill, not thought to live.

I vividly recall my mother waving good-bye to me through the glass screen. (I must have been in an isolation unit.)

Then she hurriedly turned away to hide her tears, but I knew. And then she was gone. And I cried. Fearful, alone.

I caught sight of a set of headphones beside the bed connected to the hospital radio system. I put them on and heard a song which instantly comforted me. It was "You're the Only Star in My Blue Heaven."

Suddenly, she was back with me. I was not alone. I remember smiling.

I sang that song, as best as I could remember it – and I remembered it well – many times during my three months in the hospital. It was way back then that I discovered the therapeutic power of music – the remembrance, the reassurance, of the mother most loving.

And as she lay in coma, I sang her song back to her. She was not alone. I was there – and so was her mother.

My mother never played an instrument, and I think that perhaps just once I heard her sing.

In my teens, when I asked her, she would sit by me as I played my records. And then tolerate me fatuously expounding on them. But I knew she did it out of love for me, not for music.

Over the years I would wonder where my great love for music came from. And, finally, through her dementia I found her as the source.

If only I could have helped her to play and sing, as I have done for years with so many strangers.

But it was not to be our way. Never a duet.

However, I came to know that we shared the love. And more: that my love was hers passed on.

$\mathcal{I}$'d watch her hands – tapping, tapping, always tapping.

Pointless, meaningless, brainless? Or her playing of the Music within her?

I believe it was the latter, for when I played music to her, often her tapping would change.

Yes, Music, the inner music, is about the last to die.

$\mathscr{I}$ have heard it said that it is difficult to die in the presence of a loved one, for your Spirit feels the need to hold on to the earthly existence out of concern for the loved one.

I spent virtually the last three days and nights of her life by her bedside. I left on only one occasion – to walk to the maternity hospital in which I was born and to stare up at the window of the room where she had pointed to me she had brought me into the world.

But the rest of the time I was with her as she now was leaving for another world. I was present at her death, as she had been at my birth. We were at both, together.

I sat there with her for hours on end unable to understand how a body so frail, with a brain so grossly impaired, could survive so long in coma.

Early one morning the nurses asked me to wait in the next room while they changed her position in the bed. I had no sooner left than they came to me to tell me she had died.

Her Spirit could finally leave, having stayed on, seemingly as if over its time, out of love for me.

At the funeral everyone spoke about her in the past tense, as if she had actually died ten years before and was only now being interred. To me it was the very opposite – as if, through her illness, She, the true her, the Soul within her body, had at last manifested Itself strongly, and increasingly more strongly, in the world.

I did not want to pass over the last decade – instead I wanted to, in a way, rejoice for her, and us, because of it. Yes, her disease was horrible, and her suffering, at least initially, and her family's too. But her Soul had an opportunity to prosper, to grow, and, I believe, mine with it too.

This is the message I would like to give to the loved ones of an Alzheimer's patient. There is another way of looking at the illness and the patient – and there is another way of, through it, looking at ourselves.

I've been informed that in a nursing home nearby resides a man whom I regard as one of the greatest poets of this century. He is said now to be far gone into Alzheimer's disease, and sits all day in one of those rubber chairs staring blankly.

They say he is completely inaccessible, and certainly has lost any knowledge or interest in poetry, even his own. But I know that if I hold his hands and look into his eyes, deeply into them, there I will find the Spirit that inspired the poet. It is still there. And It is now so much more apparent than It ever could have been in his poems, for now there is no ego to get in the way.

Part of my work is to train volunteers to go into nursing homes and work with the elderly and the demented. We do it through the vehicle of music, but that's not really necessary – the important thing, the only one that really matters, is to help them to know, in some way, that we know they are Spirit, whatever their present ego condition.

And by this process we too are enriched, for, as I have said before, to find the Spirit in the other is the way to find it in ourselves. And this is especially easy when, with the ego stripped away, the Spirit is so apparent.

We have taken children into nursing homes, and I will never forget them lovingly going up to demented old people and brightly, smilingly, taking their hands, looking into their eyes and singing – Soul to Soul. They helped the patients – but, even more, they were helped by them.

One day they will find a cure for Alzheimer's disease and this will be a blessing for mankind.

But we will always need visitations to help us to realize in our hearts that we are Blessed, and are ourselves capable of Blessing.

$\mathcal{M}$any seekers travel to a distant land, to a remote mountain top, to sit with a Wise Man. He may not talk, may not acknowledge their presence – may not even be aware that they are there.

But because he has surrendered his ego, they will Know his Spirit so revealed, and through his, will find an intimation of their own.

And they can find it too in the demented – but with more difficulty, for here the ego is not discarded but decayed.

Perhaps one day my relatives and friends will come to sit with me to find what I could not reveal when normal.

Perhaps I will become a Wise Man through my dementia, a Sage by default.

$\mathcal{T}$he last gift a parent has to offer is to, by example, help his children overcome their fear of death.

I used to think that a dement couldn't, for to do this, brain was required.

But I came to gratefully realize that, in her own way, my mother did give me an example, a very beautiful one. And this required not brain, but heart.

$\mathcal{Y}$ou walk into the nursing home, and there you see your mother – withdrawn, huddled, shrunken, useless. A nothing. What's the point of her existence?

But then with a new perspective (from the Latin word to see), you now behold her – literally, you reach out and grasp her, hold her, with your eyes. For you have started to see her differently.

And from this comes a new respect (from the same Latin word). You now regard her (again, the basic meaning is to see) with "honor and esteem." You have come to see her as being More than she appears to your eyes.

In her iris, you can see the joys and the pain. You can sense her as the physical. The word *iris* comes from the Greek word meaning a rainbow. And Iris was a messenger from the gods. Thus, the iris a rainbow message from the God, the Soul within the eye.

You can then go beyond the iris into the pupil. The word *pupil* comes from the Latin *pupilla*, a little doll. So called because when you look at another's pupil you see your own image reflected back in miniature.

But then look deeper, past the reflection, beyond the physical, into the world of the metaphysical, and you will "see" the other's Soul – not tiny, but Infinite. And in There, sense The Soul.

And as you continue to look into, It comes out to you, as you. You, too, are Soul.

Out of this comes a feeling of reverence, "profound awe and respect", as you see her as Soul. (And reverence, too, is to do with seeing, from the root meaning to perceive.)

These feelings of respect leading to reverence are associated with vision, with the eye and the inner eye.

And now from the eyes to the heart – from reverence to veneration. From your eyes to your heart, through her eyes to her Soul.

And veneration has a very different deeper meaning, for it is from the Latin *vener*, love – hence Venus.

At last, you can truly, totally, love her, for you now Know her as Love.

Through your new perspective, you have come to Veneration.

Her existence, you now realize, is best expressed by an old quotation: "All that is left, is only a kind of Veneration of a Being more excellent than our own."

But through her, through your veneration of her, you will come to realize that you, too, are Soul, that you, too, are Venerable.

Through your apparently useless mother, you can come to see yourself as Soul. This is her last gift of love to you.

Now, finally, you are at peace with your own existence.

Alzheimer's patients can be very disturbed, and disturbing. But every health-carer should have, must have, Veneration for every patient.

It is This that transforms them from mere treaters into healers. For healers are not just concerned with the body, but also with the Spirit.

The disease may not respond to treatment, but the Spirit will always respond to healing.

The essence of the Japanese tea ceremony is the acceptance of the As Is: to attain a state of detachment transcending judgement, when things, people, all events, all of existence, are accepted just as they are.

And this is through the recognition of the unique, yet universal, Thusness of every thing, of every person. Starting with the tea house surroundings, the tea house itself, the guests, the tea master, his utensils, and the tea. And the tea cups. They are of a particular ancient pottery tradition called raku. By the very nature of their throwing, glazing and firing, they can never be perfect in the usual sense. Always irregular – rejects in other unknowing traditions.

In the tea ceremony, the guest puts his mind into the very essence of the cup, deeper, much deeper, than its superficial appearance. There he finds its Thusness – and through this his own.

I often think of my mother as raku. In one tradition, a reject; but in another much wiser one, a source of infinite contemplation and enlightenment.

I never cried during my mother's illness, nor at her death. Nor later at my daughter Kathie's funeral.

I had come to understand that tears are for unfulfilled fantasy: what I had imagined the rest of their lives would have, should have, been. What they would have done, what we would have done together.

All tears, like all fears, are only for fantasies.

If only we can accept, gratefully, the Reality, the As Is, the Course of each life, then there is no need for fantasy – and so no tears.

A Letter From My Niece

I never knew Nanny was "there." Whenever I'd visit she would be sitting somewhere in the nursing home alone, but always near a radio. Nanny would be stroking her hand up and down her leg rhythmically. I would sit down next to her holding her hand, and she would immediately look straight into my eyes and smile that familiar warm smile and sometimes even laugh!

This reaction, whether I understood the disease or not, made me feel that much stronger about some sort of connection between Music and touch. I continued visiting Nanny as much as I could, sometimes bringing my guitar to play to her.

I now understand where that connection is for those who have Alzheimer's after reading my uncle's "new perspective." I only wish I knew then what I know now. I also hope people who are emotionally attached to these people see Uncle John's point of view, so as not to be selfish and enjoy the Spirit of the Music within the Soul.

I remember one time visiting Nanny when my Dad came in. I could see in his eyes the love he had for Nanny, but also a fear of the unknown.

He looked at me and beckoned me to leave with him, and as I looked up his eyes had filled with tears.

I remember an overwhelming feeling of love and sadness at what this disease was doing to Nanny. I now only wish Dad knew then what I understand today.

Thanks, Uncle John.

Cassandra Diamond

*A*re all with Alzheimer's like my mother? So I have found – you just have to see them as Souls.

And, through them, to so see everyone.

Most relatives are reluctant to visit – and reluctant to relate when they do.

But when they see them as Souls, they come instead with reverence and veneration.

And they leave with a new perspective on Alzheimer's and, through it, on all disease.

And more: a deeper understanding and acceptance of their own lives, of the totality of their existence.

Did she change
or did her last years
give me the chance
to really see her
for the first time?

The Creative Imperative

Meeting the
Real Health Care Needs
of the Elderly

Creativity:
the Golden Thread
to the Soul

$\mathscr{E}$nter a nursing home – and feel the fear in the walls. See it in the residents' eyes, and in the staff's. And then know it in your own heart. The fear of death, and its other face – the rejection of life.

Then hold their hands, look into their eyes, deeply – down to their souls. Sing to their souls, and encourage them to sing to yours. And all the fear goes – for a time.

What are their needs? To find their souls – to sing, and sing. They need to sing, and they need to sing to others. This is their, and our, Creative Imperative. This satisfies two basic needs: the need to express creatively, and the need to selflessly give the creativity. From soul to soul.

How to live with the specter of approaching death, and how to accept, gratefully, joyously, the inevitable – this is the health care need of the elderly.

And more: how to then teach the next generation by example. How they can best live, and die. With grace and gratitude.

And both of these needs, really the same, can, I believe, be best accomplished through the Arts.

$\mathcal{A}$rt can be a cry for help, a call or challenge for change – or a song of jubilation.

All are important. My particular work is to encourage the jubilation, the True Art.

I used to practice medicine, and complementary medicine, and psychiatry. But now I'd like to believe that I've graduated to become a member of what Freud called "a new profession of minister of souls."

Or, more accurately, a minister to the ego to help it find the Soul. For the endpoint of all my clinical experience is that only this Realization will at last overcome the universal anguish of human existence.

To become Freud's "new minister of souls," one must know his Freud. And all of psychoanalysis and clinical psychology goes back to the earliest mother-child relationship. There are the roots of our attitudes to life and death.

We are conceived and carried within the mother, born through her, nurtured and reared by her. She was in the beginning our whole world – and, at base, always remains so.

How I believe the world, any part of it, feels towards me will relate to how I feel, and felt, my mother felt towards me.

We can accept any and all events in our existence if we believe our mothers love us. For, as I say, she was, and still is, all the world to us.

Every night we leave this world to return to her womb, the other world we somehow still sense – and seek. Every night we re-enter her inner darkness.

And death is Eugene O'Neill's "Long Day's Journey into Night;" it is Raymond Chandler's "The Big Sleep."

It is Shakespeare's "Our little life is rounded with a sleep." And the roundness can remind us of pregnancy, of being inside her – again.

How we feel about life, and death, depends on how loved – or not – we feel by our mother, our first "God." Thus, to me, True Health is Knowing in our hearts the True Love of our mothers.

To find This is the most important task for the elderly, and for us all.

As we age, we come more to resemble our mothers, as they came more and more to resemble theirs. And we come more to understand them, to accept them. Hopefully to find, at last, in them, and thus in ourselves, what Freud called the Eternal Eros, Ever-Constant Love.

Thus we come to finally accept life – and death. And then our anguish is over.

I have found that the easiest way, the most efficient and effective way of approaching this seemingly unattainable goal is through the Arts. Hence I founded The Institute for Music and Health and The Arts-Health Institute.

Health, to me, is so much more than the relief of pain, even than the absence of illness. For it far transcends the physical.

It is the triumphant release, at last, from the universal anguish of human existence.

It is the joyous and grateful total acceptance of life with all of its vicissitudes – and the equally joyous and grateful acceptance of its cessation.

It is the blind St. Francis opening his eyes, and heart, to the doctor's red-hot cautery: "Come, Brother Fire!"

It is Bach, also blind, on his deathbed, knowing he will never rise again, dictating his last and holiest work, BWV 668, "Lord God, I stand before Thy Throne."

It is the exultant Blake, also on his deathbed, making a last drawing of his beloved Kate. Then, having done, singing jubilantly of the Heaven to come. He died in Perfect Health.

$\mathcal{H}$ealth, True Health, is Knowing in the heart (for it can never be known in the brain), the answers to the two questions, really one, that confront, challenge, and terrify every human being:

Who am I? and *Why am I here?*

Health, True Health, is at last, the blessed, blissful, relief from anguish – from the inability, despite all our despairing endeavors, to find our Souls.

Thus Health is: I have a Soul. And more: I am Soul.

That is Who I am. And that is Why I am here. That is the purpose, the very reason, for my existence: to become aware of my Soul, to be One with It. And to manifest It into the world for the service of other souls.

This is the greatest, the most urgent, the most important, in fact, the only Real health care need of the elderly – as it is for those of every age.

The anguish of the aged is for all of us. It is most obvious, and pressing for them as they despair of their time running out before they have overcome it, before they have, at long last, found the Peace on the earth they are about to leave.

Looking back, has there been meaning to my life? Has it meaning now – and will it ever? And has it meaning to those I will be leaving behind?

Until he finds the meaning he will fear death. And he will pass that fear on to the next generation – as it was passed on to him.

So, how to find one's Soul – that is the most important question, the only Real question. And the need to answer it becomes ever more urgent with every passing year.

But how can we go inside our selves, our egos, to find our Soul when we have spent our whole lives avoiding this very process, out of the deluded fear that inside we will find not our Goodness, our Godliness, but the very opposite?

This is where Creativity, the Arts, are so important, so essential. True Art is the golden thread to the Soul. If we follow it back we find, at last, our Souls. Go first into the song you are singing, and then into its composer; go into the apple you are painting, the tree you are photographing. Find first the Soul there.

Then go into your self and find the fountainhead, the wellspring, of your Creativity – the Muse within you. And your Muse is your Soul.

And now give your Art to those who need to find their Souls. Be an example: let your Muse help them, through them first finding your soul, to then find their own.

And through this altruistic artistic endeavor, your Soul is at last content, for It has helped other Souls. And now, at last, your anguish is over.

This is the Real health care need of the elderly: the opportunity and encouragement that, through finding their Souls through their Art, they may by altruistic service help others to find theirs. Thus their last years may not be a meaningless, valueless wasteland, but the time of their greatest benefit to all who receive their Art.

And more than just their Art, for through it they become living examples of the Muse. As will those coming behind them who see them now not as nothings, but as Manifestations – as Epiphanies.

The True Health care needs of the elderly, as for all of us, are best served and best expressed not by getting – but by giving.

Health, True Health, by my definition, is advanced by Altruism – whenever we selflessly help another. Thus the Health care needs of the elderly are best met by encouraging them to help those coming behind them.

The deeper need is not to get love, but to give it. For Altruism is health, True Health. And the Arts can be a wonderful vehicle for Altruism.

The best way, probably the only way, to find your Soul is to altruistically help another to find his. And I believe the best means whereby this can take place is through the Arts, for they so obviously and so immediately come from the Soul.

Ill-health is the shrinking into the self, encapsulation; whereas True Health is Expansion, the emanation of the Soul into the world. And Music, True Music, of all modalities, most encourages – more, exhorts – Expansion.

In Hamburg, a blind man in his nineties, doubled over with spondylitis, sits by a drum. He seems completely immobile, as if dead. But then I notice that with one finger on the drum he is tapping out the rhythms of our songs. I point this out to his nurse who exclaims, "That's the only music he's made in thirty years here!" That was the need he was expressing – after thirty years.

At a neurological hospital in London a brain-damaged paralyzed woman is placed into a wheelchair, her head held up by an extension. She can't speak or move, except one arm. With it she motions me over to her and then sort of points to her chest. Eventually I realize she wants me to put my hand on it. And I'm amazed to feel the vibrations of the song the rest are singing.

Inside she is singing! She is alive, really alive! And she smiles, as best she can. I look into her eyes and see her Soul. As she looks into me and sees mine. At that moment, we were bonded Soul to Soul. As we still are.

Contrast that example with this one from a very expensive nursing home in Zurich, with every apparent health care being provided.

A group of old ladies were seated around an occupational therapy table, all half-heartedly knitting or embroidering. I congratulated one on her ninetieth birthday. She glared right into my eyes, and almost spat out, "I'd sooner be dead." And with that all the others agreed.

All the health care they needed – but no Health care.

The old man in an intensive care ward the day after nine hours of emergency surgery. Tubes everywhere. Can't speak – tracheostomy. And so many machines to monitor his heart, but not his Heart. He's surrendered – wants to die.

I place a little egg-shaped rhythm shaker in each pale wrinkled hand. I sing and he plays with me. A duet. He smiles. He wants to live.

I don't know about his EKG – I can't read them anymore – but I do know about his Heart.

My mother, deep into Alzheimer's, would pass every day in a chair ceaselessly tapping her thigh and incessantly muttering. A sign of dementia – or was it?

I would play old records to her, the ones I played when young, and her eyes would light up. Then the tapping would change. And often when I sang to her, or played the castanets, it would stop altogether, as if not needed.

There also was the time my wife got her up out of the chair and "dancing" and asked her if she

liked it. Back came my mother's instant reply –
loud, strong, passionate. (And she hadn't spoken
for months.) "It's marvelous!"

All that tapping – all that need communicated.
But who listened?

And in her final coma I sang to her the song
that I sang to myself about her fifty years before
when I was in a hospital, thought to be dying:
"You're the Only Star in My Blue Heaven." And
somewhere, somehow, I know she heard me. And
sang with me.

What a change comes over her when I get the
frail old lady slumped in a wheelchair to start
thinking out to the young nursing aide who is
haunted by the fear that she too will one day end
up the same.

How wonderful, how epiphanic, when she
comes to life, opens her eyes and her heart, and
smiles and sings down through the generations.

In Australia, the Institute for Music and Health trains young school children to go into nursing homes and sing with the pure love that only innocent children dare to express. And most of the residents give it back, just as openly. The music a mutual circle of love.

$\mathcal{T}$he greatest Health care need is the opportunity to give love from the Soul – and this can be met by True Art most bounteously and gloriously, for It comes from the Soul: As Beethoven wrote, "From the Heart may it go to the Heart."

The more Creative, the Truer the Art, the more it expresses not just the problem (and, at base, the problem is always the same – the anguish of existence) – but also its surmounting.

We need to encourage the elderly to express not just their anguish – but also its joyous and triumphant overcoming. Their Highest Creativity.

They need to do this – for themselves, and for us. And we need them to do it for us. And we need to let them know that we need them to do it.

The word altruism is from the Latin, *alter*, other. It is said that at the very moment of the altruistic act there is no other, one becomes one with the other. The fireman braving the flames to rescue the trapped child – oneness.

This I believe – and more. That our lives should be not just occasional altruistic events, but a continuous progression of altruism, from moment to moment throughout our existence. Our lives themselves as Altruism.

Then, so I am led to believe, we become not just one with the one other, but with all others. All One, all One with The One.

This must be the way to live, and to die.

And this, and nothing less than this, is the Creative Imperative.

A Plan for the Elderly to Express
The Creative Imperative

*I*n every community there is a large number of the elderly who need Music, and all the Arts.

And there is in that same community an equal number of the elderly who want to give it, who need to give it – if only they knew how, were taught how.

Every community needs a coordinator, a facilitator, to bring these two needing parties together. Each needing to give and receive Music – each needing to find their souls through finding them in the other. Mutual Altruism.

Epilogue

*T*rue Art, the Art of Aspiration and of Altruism, the Song of Love for the Love, is still but a hope for the future. It has, so I believe, yet to exist on earth – or at least in our society.

We have no instruments made specifically for this Art, no body of music composed for It – if composed music is the way, anyway.

And, most tragically, we have no examples of It that we can emulate. For our society has yet to make this a major priority: the overcoming of the human condition by the surrendering of the ego for the advancement of the soul – rather than, seemingly increasingly, mere ego gratification.

When that day comes – as it must if we are to survive – True Art will be accorded its rightful place as a most powerful Force to alleviate the anguish of the human condition.

Until then, all we can do is, to a very limited extent, explore, and explain, and encourage. To give the merest intimation.

Summary

The last duty of the elderly is to set an example – how to live, and how to die.

This they want to learn, and need to learn – and this they want to teach, and need to teach.

This is their, and our, greatest Health care need.

To die
never having released
the Music inside you
is indeed a tragedy
– for you,
and for us.

John Diamond, M.D.

Dr. John Diamond, M.D., D.P.M., F.R.A.N.Z.C.P., M.R.C.Psych., F.I.A.P.M., D.I.B.A.K., graduated from Sydney University Medical School in 1957, and was awarded his Diploma in Psychological Medicine in 1962. He is a Fellow of the Royal Australian and New Zealand College of Psychiatry, and a Foundation Member of the Royal College of Psychiatrists as well as a Member of The American Holistic Medical Association, The International Arts-Medicine Association and The Society for the Arts in Healthcare.

After practicing psychiatry for a number of years, he expanded into complementary medicine, becoming President of the International Academy of Preventive Medicine in the United States. As a Holistic Consultant, Dr. Diamond is concerned with all aspects of the totality of the sufferer – body, mind and spirit – how they relate and how all must be involved in every Healing process. He has for many years also used Creativity to help sufferers, regarding it as an essential and major component of healing.

Dr. Diamond's approach to disease and suffering is based on his extensive clinical experience in medicine, psychiatry, complementary medicine, the humanities, holistic healing, and the arts.

For further information, please contact:

The Diamond Center
P. O. Box 381
South Salem, New York   10590
(914) 533-2158

www.diamondcenter.net
Email: mail@diamondcenter.net